ABOUT THE BOOK AND HOW TO READ IT:

The book has been made for a possible more intuitive way to learn fast the Italian language. You will recognize your language with a specific colour before a sentence started and this colour will be the same for all the rest of your native language sentences, in which it helps to locate your mother language quick, and for the new learning language you will see that it is highlight with a different colour to don't mix up both languages. When you see the square brackets […], that means you need to find out the word you want to use on your native language and it depends on your personal situation, for example: (a flight number is something personal), and you need to add it at your sentence. You also will find out how to count to 10, that are the most essential numbers you need with you, remember that the book no mentions the full numerical numbers but only the one you need for your vacation. Every real holiday situation is separated by chapters and each chapter contain 20 phrases; and its picture related which you can recall your situation just viewing the index chapters and pages numbered.

CHAPTERS:

Chapter 1) ITALIAN PRONUNCIATION

Italian pronunciation is generally phonetic, which means that words are pronounced as they are spelled. Here is a brief overview of Italian pronunciation:

1. Vowels:

a: similar to "a" in "car"

e: similar to "e" in "bed"

i: similar to "ee" in "see"

o: similar to "o" in "go"

u: similar to "oo" in "food"

2. Consonants: b, c, d, f, g, h, l, m, n, p, q, s, t, v, z:

Pronounced as in English.

ch: similar to "k" in "kite"

g (before e and i): similar to "j" in "jeep"

gn: similar to the "ny" in "canyon"

r: rolled or flipped, similar to the Spanish "r"

s (between vowels or after a consonant): pronounced "z" as in "haze"

sc (before e and i): similar to "sh" in "sheep"

z: similar to "ts" in "hats"

3. Double Consonants:

Double consonants are pronounced more forcefully than single consonants. For example, "t" in "citta" is pronounced with a slightly stronger emphasis than in "cita."

4. **Accent:**

Italian words are stressed on the second-to-last syllable if the word ends in a vowel, and on the last syllable if the word ends in a consonant. There are exceptions, and some words have an accent mark to indicate stress.

5. **Diphthongs:**

Italian has fewer diphthongs than English. Two vowel letters next to each other are usually pronounced separately. For example, "ai" in "Italia" is pronounced as two separate vowels.

6. **Common Pronunciation Challenges:**

English speakers might find it helpful to practice the rolled "r" sound and to be aware of the pronunciation of certain combinations like "gli," which is pronounced like "ll" in the English word "million."

7. **Nasal Vowels:**

Italian does not have nasal vowels like in French, so vowels are generally pronounced with the mouth open.

8. **Silent Letters:**

Italian is relatively phonetic, but there are instances where certain letters are silent. For example, the final "e" in many words is often silent.

It's important to note that regional accents exist in Italy, and pronunciation can vary somewhat from region to region. Listening to native speakers and practicing with them can greatly help in improving your Italian pronunciation.

Chapter 2) AT THE AIRPORT

Here are 20 phrases in Italian that you might find useful when you are at the airport:

1. Asking for Directions:

English: "Excuse me, where is the departure gate for [your flight number]?"

Italian: "Mi scusi, dov'è il gate di partenza per il volo [……….]?"

2. Checking in at the Counter:

English: "I have a reservation for [your name]."

Italian: "Ho una prenotazione a nome di [………….]."

3. Security Check:

English: "Where is the security checkpoint?"
Italian: "Dove si trova il controllo di sicurezza?"

4. Boarding the Plane:

English: "What time does the flight to [your destination] board?"

Italian: "A che ora imbarca il volo per [……………..]?"

5. Asking about Delays:

English: "Is there any delay for the flight to [your destination]?"

Italian: "C'è qualche ritardo per il volo per [……………..]?"

6. In the Duty-Free Shop:

English: "How much is this item?"

Italian: "Quanto costa questo articolo?"

7. At the Information Desk:

English: "Can you help me find my gate?"

Italian: "Può aiutarmi a trovare il mio gate?"

8. Getting a Taxi at the Airport:

English: "I need a taxi to [my destination]."

Italian: "Ho bisogno di un taxi per [………….]."

9. At the Baggage Claim:

English: "Where can I find the baggage claim for the flight [your flight number]?"
Italian: "Dove posso trovare il ritiro bagagli per il volo [….]?"

10. Inquiring about Facilities:

English: "Where are the toilets?"

Italian: "Dove sono i servizi igienici?"

11. At the Currency Exchange:

English: "What is the exchange rate for euros to [your currency]?"
Italian: "Qual è il tasso di cambio per gli euro in [………….]?"

12. Seeking Assistance:

English: "I need help with my luggage."

Italian: "Ho bisogno di aiuto con i bagagli."

13. At the Information Desk:

English: "Can you provide information about local transportation from the airport?"
Italian: "Può fornire informazioni sui trasporti locali dall'aeroporto?"

14. At the Food Court:

English: "I would like a [specific food or drink]."

Italian: "Vorrei un [……………]."

15. In Case of Emergency:

English: "Where is the nearest medical facility?"

Italian: "Dove si trova la struttura medica più vicina?"

16. Asking about Wi-Fi:

English: "Is there free Wi-Fi at the airport?"

Italian: "C'è Wi-Fi gratuito all'aeroporto?"

17. Expressing Concerns:

English: "I can't find my boarding pass. What should I do?"

Italian: "Non trovo la mia carta d'imbarco. Cosa devo fare?"

18. At the Lost and Found:

English: "I forgot something on the plane. Where is the lost and found office?"

Italian: "Ho dimenticato qualcosa sull'aereo. Dove si trova l'ufficio oggetti smarriti?"

19. Navigating the Airport:

English: "How do I get to the [specific area or gate] from here?"

Italian: "Come posso arrivare a […………………..] da qui?"

20. Expressing Gratitude:

English: "Thank you for your help."

Italian: "Grazie per l'aiuto."

Chapter 3) IN THE TAXI

Here are 20 phrases in Italian that you might find useful when you are in a taxi:

1. Giving Directions:

English: "Please take me to [your destination]."

Italian: "Per favore, portatemi a [……….…].''

2. Asking about the Fare:

English: "How much does the ride to [your destination] cost?"

Italian: "Quanto costa il viaggio fino a [………..]?"

3. Asking for a Receipt:

English: "Can I have a receipt, please?"

Italian: "Posso avere una ricevuta, per favore?"

4. Asking for Recommendations:

English: "Do you have any recommendations for good restaurants around here?"

Italian: "Ha qualche raccomandazione per buoni ristoranti in zona?"

5. Checking if the Taxi Accepts Credit Cards:

English: "Do you accept credit cards?"

Italian: "Accettate carte di credito?"

6. Expressing Urgency:

English: "Please hurry, I have a flight to catch."

Italian: "Per favore, sbrigatevi, devo prendere il volo."

7. Asking about the Route:

English: "Is this the fastest way to [your destination]?"

Italian: "È questa la strada più veloce per arrivare a [………..]?"

8. Expressing Gratitude:

English: "Thank you for the ride."

Italian: "Grazie per il passaggio."

9. Asking for Assistance:

English: "Could you help me with my luggage, please?"

Italian: "Potrebbe aiutarmi con i bagagli, per favore?"

10. Confirming the Drop-off Location:

English: "Please drop me off at [specific location]."

Italian: "Mi può lasciare a [………..], per favore?"

11. Asking about the Duration of the Ride:

English: "How long will it take to get to [your destination]?"

Italian: "Quanto tempo ci vorrà per arrivare a [………….]?"

12. Asking about Traffic:

English: "Is there a lot of traffic on the way to [your destination]?"

Italian: "C'è molto traffico sulla strada per [………….]?"

13. Requesting a Specific Route:

English: "Could you take the scenic route, please?"

Italian: "Potrebbe prendere la strada panoramica, per favore?"

14. Asking for Air Conditioning or Heating:

English: "Could you please turn on the air conditioning?"

Italian: "Potrebbe accendere l'aria condizionata, per favore?"

15. Asking for the Taxi Driver's Card:

English: "May I have your card, please?"

Italian: "Posso avere la sua carta, per favore?"

16. Confirming the Fare:

English: "Is the fare metered or fixed for this trip?"

Italian: "Il costo è a tariffa o fisso per questo viaggio?"

17. Expressing Appreciation for a Smooth Ride:

English: "Thank you for the smooth ride."

Italian: "Grazie per il viaggio confortevole."

18. Asking for Assistance with Payment:

English: "Can you help me break a large bill?"

Italian: "Può aiutarmi a cambiare una banconota grande?"

19. Asking for a Business Card:

English: "Do you have a business card?"

Italian: "Ha una carta da visita?"

20. **Asking for a Recommendation:**

English: "Can you recommend a good place to visit

around here?"

Italian: "Può consigliare un bel posto da visitare in zona?"

These phrases should help you communicate effectively with the
taxi driver in Italy.

Chapter 4) AT THE HOTEL

Here are 20 phrases in Italia

n that you might find useful when you are at the hotel:

1. Checking In:

English: "Good evening, I have a reservation under [name]."

Italian: "Buonasera, ho una prenotazione a nome di [………]."

2. Asking about Room Availability:

English: "Is the room ready?"

Italian: "La camera è pronta?"

3. Asking for a Different Room:

English: "Could I have a room with a [specific request]?"

Italian: "Potrei avere una camera con […………]?"

4. Inquiring about Hotel Facilities:

English: Does the hotel have facilities like gym and restaurant?"

Italian: "Ha l'hotel strutture come la palestra e il ristorante?"

5. Asking for Wi-Fi Access:

English: "Could you provide the Wi-Fi password, please?"

Italian: "Potrebbe fornire la password del Wi-Fi, per favore?"

6. Requesting Additional Amenities:

English: "Could I have extra towels, please?"
Italian: "Potrei avere degli asciugamani da toeletta aggiuntivi, per favore?"

7. Inquiring about Breakfast:

English: "Is breakfast included in the room rate?"

Italian: "La colazione è inclusa nella tariffa della camera?"

8. Asking for Local Recommendations:

English: "Can you recommend any good restaurants or attractions nearby?"
Italian: "Può consigliare qualche buon ristorante o attrazioni nelle vicinanze?"

9. Reporting an Issue in the Room:

English: "There seems to be an issue with [specific problem] in my room."

Italian: "Sembra ci sia un problema con [.....] nella mia camera."

10. Asking about Check-Out Time:

English: "What time is check-out tomorrow?"

Italian: "A che ora è il check-out domani?"

11. Expressing Gratitude:

English: "Thank you for your assistance."

Italian: "Grazie per l'aiuto."

12. Requesting a Wake-Up Call:

English: "Could I have a wake-up call at [specific time] tomorrow?"

Italian: "Potrei avere una chiamata alle [………] domani?"

13. Asking for a Map:

English: "Could I have a map of the local area?"

Italian: "Potrei avere una mappa della zona locale?"

14. Inquiring about the Hotel's Policy:

English: "What is the hotel's policy on [specific request]?"

Italian: "Qual è la politica dell'hotel riguardo a [………..]?"

15. Asking for Assistance with Luggage:

English: "Could someone help me with my luggage, please?"

Italian: "Qualcuno potrebbe aiutarmi con i bagagli, per favore?"

16. Requesting Room Cleaning:

English: "Could you please clean my room?"

Italian: "Potrebbe per favore pulire la mia camera?"

17. Asking for a Taxi:

English: "Could you call a taxi for me?"

Italian: "Potrebbe chiamare un taxi per me, per favore?"

18. Asking about Local Transportation:

English: "How can I get to [specific location] using public transport?"

Italian: "Come posso arrivare a [………….] con i mezzi pubblici?"

19. Checking Out:

English: "I'd like to check out, please."

Italian: "Vorrei fare il check-out, per favore."

20. Leaving Feedback:

English: "I enjoyed my stay. Thank you."

Italian: "Ho apprezzato il mio soggiorno. Grazie."

Feel free to use these phrases during your stay at a hotel in Italy, adjusting them based on your specific needs and situations.

Chapter 5) AT THE RESTAURANT

Here are 20 phrases in Italian that you might find useful when you are in a restaurant:

1. Requesting a Table:

English: "Table for [number of people], please."

Italian: "Un tavolo per […………], per favore."

2. Asking for the Menu:

English: "May I see the menu, please?"

Italian: "Posso vedere il menù, per favore?"

3. Ordering Drinks:

English: "I would like a [specific drink], please."

Italian: "Vorrei un [………..], per favore."

4. **Ordering Food:**

English: "I'll have this dish, please."

Italian: "Prenderò questo piatto, per favore."

5. **Asking for Recommendations:**

English: "What do you recommend?"

Italian: "Cosa consiglia?"

6. **Checking for Allergens:**

English: "Does this dish contain [specific allergen]?"

Italian: "Questo piatto contiene [………….]?"

7. **Requesting Modifications:**

English: "Could I have an extra dish?"

Italian: "Potrei avere un piatto aggiuntivo?"

8. **Inquiring about Specials dish:**

English: "Are there any specials dish recommendations today?"
Italian: "Ci sono dei piatti speciali oggi che puo' raccomandarmi?"

9. **Asking for Bread or Condiments:**

English: "Could we have some bread and olive oil, please?"

Italian: "Potremmo avere del pane e dell'olio d'oliva, per favore?"

10. **Expressing Appreciation for the Meal:**

English: "The meal is delicious, thank you."

Italian: "Il pasto è delizioso, grazie."

11. Asking for the Bill:

English: "Can we have the bill, please?"

Italian: "Possiamo avere il conto, per favore?"

12. Complimenting the Chef:

English: "Compliments to the chef. The food is excellent."

Italian: "Complimenti allo chef. Il cibo è eccellente."

13. Asking for Tap Water:

English: "May we have some tap water, please?"

Italian: "Possiamo avere dell'acqua del rubinetto, per favore?

14. Asking for the Wi-Fi Password:

English: "Could you provide the Wi-Fi password, please?"

Italian: "Potrebbe fornire la password del Wi-Fi, per favore?"

15. Asking for a Dog Bag:

English: "Could I have a dog bag, please?"
Italian: "Potrei avere una borsa per cani?"

16. Checking Opening Hours:

English: "What time do you close?"

Italian: "A che ora chiudete?"

17. Expressing Dietary Restrictions:

English: "I'm (vegetarian/vegan). Do you have any options?"

Italian: "Sono (vegetariano/vegano). Avete opzioni per me?"

18. Inquiring about Spice Level:

English: "Is this dish spicy?"

Italian: "Questo piatto è piccante?"

19. Asking for Dessert:

English: "What desserts do you have?"

Italian: "Quali dolci avete?"

20. Expressing Satisfaction:

English: "We had a wonderful meal. Thank you."
Italian: "Abbiamo mangiato benissimo. Grazie."

Feel free to use these phrases during your dining experience in an Italian restaurant, adapting them based on your preferences and needs.

Chapter 6) AT THE SUPERMARKET

Here are 20 phrases in Italian

that you might find useful when you are at the supermarket:

1. Asking for Assistance:
English: "Excuse me, where can I find [specific item]?"

Italian: "Scusi, dove posso trovare […………]?"

2. Inquiring about Special Offers:

English: "Are there any special offers or discounts today?"

Italian: "Ci sono offerte speciali o sconti oggi?"

3. **Asking for Help with Finding a Product:**

English: "Could you help me locate [specific product]?"

Italian: "Potrebbe aiutarmi a trovare [………..]?"

4. **Asking about the Price:**

English: "How much does this cost?"

Italian: "Quanto costa questo?"

5. **Requesting a Shopping Cart or Basket:**

English: "May I have a shopping basket, please?"
Italian: "Posso avere un cestino della spesa, per favore?"

6. **Checking for Organic Products:**

English: "Do you have organic fruits and vegetables?"

Italian: "Avete frutta e verdura biologica?"

7. **Asking for a Receipt:**

English: "Can I get a receipt, please?"

Italian: "Posso avere la ricevuta, per favore?"

8. **Asking for a Different Size:**

English: "Do you have this in a larger or smaller size?"

Italian: "Avete questo in una taglia più grande o piccola?"

9. **Inquiring about the Freshness of Prodoucts:**

English: "How fresh are the fruits and vegetables?"

Italian: "Quanto sono freschi, la frutta e' le verdure?"

10. Asking about the Location of Checkout:

English: "Where is the checkout counter?"

Italian: "Dove si trova la cassa?"

11. Requesting Assistance with Heavy Items:

English: "Could you help me with this heavy item?"

Italian: "Potrebbe aiutarmi con questo articolo pesante?"

12. Asking for a Price Check:

English: "Could you check the price for me?"

Italian: "Potrebbe controllare il prezzo per me?"

13. Expressing Gratitude for Assistance:

English: "Thank you for your help."

Italian: "Grazie per l'aiuto."

14. Asking about the Opening Hours:

English: "What time does the supermarket close?"

Italian: "A che ora chiude il supermercato?"

15. Requesting a Plastic or Paper Bag:

English: "May I have a plastic or paper bag, please?"
Italian: "Posso avere una busta di plastica o di cartone, per favore?"

16. Inquiring about Payment Methods:

English: "Do you accept credit cards?"

Italian: "Accettate carte di credito?"

17. **Asking about a Loyalty Program:**
English: "Do you have a loyalty program or
a rewards card?"
Italian: "Avete un programma fedeltà o una carta premio?"

18. **Checking Expiry Dates:**
English: "Could you check the expiration date on this
product?"
Italian: "Potrebbe controllare la data di scadenza di questo
prodotto?"

19. **Requesting Assistance at the Deli Counter:**
English: "Could I get [specific amount] of sliced ham,
please?"
Italian: "Potrei avere [...] di prosciutto affettato, per favore?"

20. **Expressing Satisfaction with the Shopping
Experience:**
English: "I found everything I needed. Thank you."
Italian: "Ho trovato tutto quello che mi serviva. Grazie."

Feel free to use these phrases during your shop supermarket
in Italy, adapting them based on your specific needs and
circumstances.

Chapter 7) IN THE STREET

Here are 20 phrases in Italian
you might find useful when you are in the street:

1. **Asking for Directions:**
English: "Can you tell me how to get to this [location]?"
Italian: "Mi può dire come arrivare a [.......]?"

2. **Asking for a Nearby supermarket:**

English: "Is there a supermarket nearby?"

Italian: "C'è un supermaercato nelle vicinanze?"

3. **Requesting Help with a Map:**

English: "Could you help me find this place on the map?"

Italian: "Potrebbe aiutarmi a trovare questo posto sulla mappa?"

4. **Inquiring about Local Attractions:**

English: "What are the must-see attractions around here?"

Italian: "Quali sono le attrazioni da non perdere qui vicino?"

5. **Ordering Food from Street Vendors:**

English: "I'd like to order [street food item], please."

Italian: "Vorrei ordinare [......], per favore."

6. **Asking for Recommendations:**

English: "Can you recommend a good restaurant in the area?"

Italian: "Può consigliarmi un buon ristorante in zona?"

7. **Asking about Local Events:**

English: "Are there any events happening in the city?"

Italian: "Ci sono eventi in corso in città?"

8. **Inquiring about Shopping Opportunities:**

English: "Where is the nearest shopping center market?"

Italian: "Dove si trova la un centro commerciale più vicino?"

9. **Requesting a Taxi:**

English: "Can you help me call a taxi?"

Italian: "Può aiutarmi a chiamare un taxi?"

10. **Inquiring about Public Transportation:**

English: "How do I get to the metro station?"

Italian: "Come arrivo alla stazione della metro?"

11. **Asking for Wi-Fi Information:**

English: "Is there free Wi-Fi around here?"

Italian: "C'è Wi-Fi gratuito qui intorno?"

12. **Seeking Assistance in an Emergency:**

English: "I need help. Is there a police station nearby?"
Italian: "Ho bisogno di aiuto. C'è una stazione di polizia
 nelle vicinanze?"

13. **Complimenting the Street Atmosphere:**

English: "This street is charming! I love the atmosphere."

Italian: "Questa strada è affascinante! Adoro l'atmosfera."

14. **Inquiring about Local Customs:**

English: "Are there any local customs I should be aware of?"

Italian: "Ci sono usanze locali di cui dovrei essere a conoscenza?"

15. **Asking for the Time:**

English: "Excuse me, do you have the time?"

Italian: "Mi scusi, ha l'ora?"

16. Requesting Assistance with Language:

English: "I'm trying to learn Italian. Can you help me practice a few phrases?"

Italian: "Sto cercando di imparare l'italiano. Può aiutarmi a praticare alcune frasi?"

17. Asking for a Recommended Walking Route:

English: "What's a good walking route to explore the city on foot?"

Italian: "Qual è un buon percorso a piedi per esplorare la città?"

18. Inquiring about Local Art Galleries:

English: "Are there any art galleries or museums in the area?"

Italian: "Ci sono gallerie d'arte o musei nella zona?"

19. Asking for Local Weather Information:

English: "How's the weather today? Is it going to rain?"

Italian: "Com'è il tempo oggi? Pioverà?"

20. Expressing Gratitude:

English: "Thank you for your help and information!"

Italian: "Grazie per l'aiuto e le informazioni!"

Feel free to use these phrases as you navigate the Italian street. They should come in handy for various situations you might encounter.

Chapter 8) AT THE COFFEE SHOP 

Here are 20 phrases in Italian

that you might find useful when you are in a coffee shop:

1. Ordering a Drink:

English: "I would like a [specific drink], please."

Italian: "Vorrei un [………], per favore."

2. Asking for the drink Menu:

English: "May I see the drink menu?"

Italian: "Posso vedere il menu delle bevande?"

3. Asking for Recommendations:

English: "What do you recommend?"

Italian: "Cosa consiglia?"

4. Requesting Water:

English: "Can I have a glass of water, please?"

Italian: "Posso avere un bicchiere d'acqua, per favore?"

5. Ordering Coffee:

English: "I'll have an espresso, please."

Italian: "Prenderò un espresso, per favore."

6. Asking for the Bill:

English: "Can we have the bill, please?"

Italian: "Possiamo avere il conto, per favore?"

7. Asking for Snacks:

English: "Do you have any snacks or appetizers?"

Italian: "Avete degli snack o dei antipasti?"

8.Asking for Ice:

English: "Could I have some ice in my drink, please?"

Italian: "Posso avere del ghiaccio nel mia bevanda, per favore?"

9.Inquiring about Happy Hour:

English: "Is there a happy hour special?"

Italian: "C'è uno speciale happy hour?"

10.Ordering Wine:

English: "I would like a glass of [specific wine], please."

Italian: "Vorrei un bicchiere di [………], per favore."

11.Expressing Appreciation for the Drink:

English: "This is delicious. Thank you."

Italian: "È delizioso. Grazie."

12.Asking for a Different Glass:

English: "Could I have this in a [specific type of glass], please?"

Italian: "Potrei avere questo in un bicchiere [……..], per favore?"

13.Inquiring about Live Music or Events:

English: "Are there any live music performances or events tonight?"

Italian: "Ci sono esibizioni di musica dal vivo o eventi stasera?"

14.Requesting a Non-Alcoholic Option:

English: "Do you have any non-alcoholic options?"

Italian: "Avete opzioni analcoliche?"

15.Ordering a Cocktail:

English: "I'll have a [specific cocktail], please."

Italian: "Prenderò un [……………], per favore."

16.Asking for the Wi-Fi Password:

English: "Could you provide the Wi-Fi password, please?"

Italian: "Potrebbe fornire la password del Wi-Fi, per favore?"

17.Asking for a Refill:

English: "Can I get a refill, please?"

Italian: "Posso avere un rabbocco, per favore?"

18.Complimenting the Atmosphere:

English: "The atmosphere here is great!"

Italian: "L'atmosfera qui è fantastica!"

19.Requesting a Bar Snack:

English: "Could I get some bar snacks, like nuts or olives?"

Italian: "Potrei avere degli snack, come noci o olive?"

20.Asking for a coffee List:

English: "May I see the coffee list?"

Italian: "Posso vedere la lista dei caffe'?"

Feel free to use these phrases in a coffee shop setting in Italy, adapting them based on your preferences and the situation.

Chapter 9) AT THE THEATRE

Here are 20 phrases in Italian

that you might find useful when you are at the theatre:

1. Buying Tickets:

English: "I would like to buy [number] tickets for [name of the play or movie]."

Italian: "Vorrei comprare [.….] biglietti per [..….]."

2. Asking about Showtimes:

English: "What time does the show start?"

Italian: "A che ora inizia lo spettacolo?"

3. Inquiring about Seat Availability:

English: "Are there any seats available for the [time of the show] performance?"

Italian: "Ci sono posti disponibili per lo spettacolo delle [...]?"

4. Asking for the Theater Location:

English: "Where is the theater located?"

Italian: "Dove si trova il teatro?"

5. Requesting a Program:

English: "Can I have a program, please?"

Italian: "Posso avere un programma, per favore?"

6. Asking about Intermission:

English: "Is there an intermission during the show?"

Italian: "C'è un intervallo durante lo spettacolo?"

7. Ordering Refreshments:

English: "I'd like to order [specific food] during the intermission."

 Italian: "Vorrei ordinare [... …..] durante l'intervallo."

8. Expressing Excitement:

English: "I'm really looking forward to the performance!"

Italian: "Non vedo l'ora di vedere lo spettacolo!"

9. Asking for Assistance with Seating:

English: "Could you help me find my seat?"

Italian: "Potrebbe aiutarmi a trovare il mio posto?"

10. Complimenting the Venue:

English: "This theater is beautiful!"

Italian: "Questo teatro è bellissimo!"

11. Inquiring about Dress Code:

English: "Is there a dress code for the theater?"

Italian: "C'è un codice di abbigliamento per il teatro?"

12. Expressing Appreciation for the Performance:

English: "The performance was outstanding!"

Italian: "La rappresentazione è stata eccezionale!"

13. Discussing the Plot:

English: "What is about the scene?"

Italian: "Di cosa tratta la scena?"

14. **Asking about Ticket Prices:**

English: "How much are the tickets for this show?"

Italian: "Quanto costano i biglietti per questo spettacolo?"

15. **Checking for Senior or Student Discounts:**

English: "Are there discounts for seniors or students?"

Italian: "Ci sono sconti per anziani o studenti?"

16. **Inquiring about Accessibility:**

English: "Is the theater accessible for people with disabilities?"

Italian: "Il teatro è accessibile alle persone con disabilità?"

17. **Requesting Quiet During the Performance:**

English: "Please remember to keep quiet during the performance."

Italian: "Per favore, ricordatevi di farre silenzio durante lo spettacolo."

18. **Asking about Parking:**

English: "Is there parking available near the theater?"

Italian: "C'è parcheggio disponibile vicino al teatro?"

19. **Requesting an Autograph or Photo:**

English: "Is it possible to get an photo with the cast after the show?"

Italian: "È possibile avere una foto con il cast dopo lo spettacolo?"

20. **Expressing Gratitude:**

English: "Thank you for a wonderful evening at the theater!"

Italian: "Grazie per una meravigliosa serata al teatro!"

Chapter 10) AT THE MUSEO

Here are 20 phrases in Italian that you might find useful when you are at the museum:

1. Buying Tickets:

English: "I would like to buy [number] tickets for the museum."

Italian: "Vorrei comprare [………] biglietti per il museo."

2. Asking about Opening Hours:

English: "What are the museum's opening hours?"

Italian: "Quali sono gli orari di apertura del museo?"

3. Inquiring about Guided Tours:

English: "Are there guided tours available?"

Italian: "Ci sono visite guidate disponibili?"

4. Asking for a Map:

English: "Could I have a map of the museum, please?"

Italian: "Posso avere una mappa del museo, per favore?"

5. Asking for Information about Exhibits:

English: "Can you tell me more about this exhibit?"

Italian: "Può dirmi qualcosa in più su questa esposizione?"

6. **Expressing Interest in Artifacts:**

English: "I'm particularly interested in artifacts. Where can I find them?"
Italian: "Sono particolarmente interessato agli artefatti. Dove posso trovarli?"

7. **Asking about Audio Guides:**

English: "Are there audio guides available for the exhibits?"

Italian: "Ci sono guide audio disponibili per le esposizioni?"

8. **Requesting Permission for Photography:**

English: "Is photography allowed in the museum?"

Italian: "È permesso fare fotografie nel museo?"

9. **Asking about Temporary Exhibitions:**

English: "Are there any temporary exhibitions currently?"

Italian: "Ci sono mostre temporanee al momento?"

10. **Inquiring about Discounts:**

English: "Are there any discounts for students or seniors?"

Italian: "Ci sono sconti per studenti o anziani?"

11. **Requesting Access to restrooms:**

English: "Where are the restrooms located?"

Italian: "Dove si trovano i servizi igienici?"

12. **Complimenting the Museum:**

English: "This museum is impressive!"

Italian: "Questo museo è impressionante!"

13. **Asking for Recommendations:**

English: "What exhibits or artworks do you recommend seeing?"

Italian: "Quali esposizioni o opere d'arte mi consiglia di vedere?"

14. **Expressing Amazement at Artwork:**

English: "The artwork here is stunning!"

Italian: "Le opere d'arte qui sono stupefacenti!"

15. **Inquiring about Educational Programs:**

English: "Are there educational programs or workshops for visitors?"

Italian: "Ci sono programmi educativi o laboratori per i visitatori?"

16. **Asking about Sculptures:**

English: "Where can I find the sculpture exhibit?"

Italian: "Dove posso trovare l'esposizione delle sculture?"

17. **Asking about Family-Friendly Activities:**

English: "Are there activities suitable for families with children?"

Italian: "Ci sono attività adatte alle famiglie con bambini?"

18. **Inquiring about the History of the Museum:**

English: "Can you tell me about the history of the museum?"

Italian: "Può parlarmi della storia del museo?"

19. **Asking for Souvenirs:**

English: "Is there a museum shop where I can buy souvenirs?"

Italian: "C'è un negozio nel museo dove posso comprare souvenir?"

20. **Expressing Gratitude:**

English: "Thank you for the information. I'm enjoying my visit."

Italian: "Grazie per le informazioni. Sto apprezzando la mia visita."

Feel free to use these phrases during your museum experience
 in Italy, adapting them based on the context and your specific needs

Chapter 11) AT THE HOSPITAL 
Here are 20 phrases in Italian
that you might find useful when you are at the hospital:

1. **Check-in at Reception:**

English: "I have an appointment with Dr. [Name]."

Italian: "Ho un appuntamento con il Dottor [….]."

2. **Providing Personal Information:**

English: "My name is [Your Name]."

Italian: "Mi chiamo [……]."

3. **Describing Symptoms:**

English: "I've been experiencing [symptoms]."

Italian: "Ho avuto questi [……]."

4. **Verifying Appointment Time:**

English: "Is my appointment at [time] confirmed?"

Italian: "Il mio appuntamento alle [.….] è confermato?"

5. Asking about Wait Time:

English: "How long is the expected wait?"

Italian: "Quanto tempo si prevede di dover aspettare?"

6. Inquiring about Test Results:

English: "Have the test results come in?"

Italian: "Sono arrivati i risultati degli esami?"

7. Requesting Explanation of Medical Terms:

English: "Could you explain that medical term to me?"

Italian: "Potrebbe spiegarmi quel termine medico?"

8. Asking for More Information about a Procedure:

English: "Can you tell me more about the [name of the procedure]?"

Italian: "Può dirmi di più sulla [………………]?"

9. Expressing Pain or Discomfort:

English: "I'm in pain/discomfort."

Italian: "Sento dolore/disagio."

10. Requesting Medication:

English: "Could I get a prescription for [medication]?"

Italian: "Potrei avere una ricetta medica per [……..]?"

11. Asking for a Second Opinion:

English: "Can I get a second opinion on my diagnosis?"

Italian: "Posso avere una seconda opinione sulla mia diagnosi?"

12. Inquiring about Visitor Policies:

English: "What are the visiting hours and policies?"

Italian: "Quali sono gli orari e le regole per I visitatori?"

13. Requesting a Copy of Medical Records:

English: "Can I get a copy of my medical records?"

Italian: "Posso ottenere una copia della mia cartella clinica?"

14. Discussing Allergies:

English: "I have allergies to [allergens]."

Italian: "Sono allergico/a a [……..]."

15. Asking about Discharge Instructions:

English: "What are the discharge instructions?"

Italian: "Quali sono le istruzioni per la dimissione?"

16. Expressing Gratitude to the Medical Staff:

English: "Thank you for your help and care."

Italian: "Grazie per l'aiuto e l'attenzione."

17. Asking for a Follow-Up Appointment:

English: "When should I schedule a follow-up appointment?"

Italian: "Quando dovrei fissare un appuntamento di controllo?"

18. Inquiring about Rehabilitation Services:

English: "Are there rehabilitation services available?"

Italian: "Ci sono servizi di riabilitazione disponibili?"

19. **Requesting a Consultation with a Specialist:**

English: "Can I request a consultation with a specialist?"

Italian: "Posso richiedere una consulenza con uno specialista?"

20. **Asking about Hospital Amenities:**

English: "Are there any amenities or services available for patients?"

Italian: "Ci sono servizi o strutture disponibili per i pazienti?"

Feel free to use these phrases in a hospital situation in Italy, adapting them based on your specific needs.

Chapter 12) ASKING ABOUT THE TIME

Here are 20 phrases

in Italian that you can use to ask about the time:

1. **Casual Inquiry:**
English: "Excuse me, do you have the time?"

Italian: "Scusi, ha l' ora?"

2. **Polite Request:**

English: "Could you please tell me the time, please?"

Italian: "Potrebbe dirmi che ore sono, per favore?"

3. **Asking a Stranger:**

English: "Sorry to bother you, but could you let me know
what time it is?"

Italian: "Scusa il disturb, ma potresti dirmi che ore sono?"

4. **Inquiring about the Hour:**

English: "What time is it right now?"

Italian: "Che ora è adesso?"

5. **Checking the Time for an Appointment:**

English: "I have an appointment. Could you tell me the time?"

Italian: "Ho un appuntamento. Potrebbe dirmi che ora è?"

6. **Requesting Time Confirmation:**

English: "Just to confirm, can you tell me the time?"

Italian: "Solo per confermare, può dirmi che ora è?"

7. **Checking the Time for a Meeting:**

English: "I'm supposed to meet someone. What time is it?"

Italian: "Supponevo di incontrare qualcuno, mi sa dire che ora è?"

8. **Inquiring about the Time Zone:**

English: "Is the time here in [location] is the same as [your home city]?"
Italian: "L'ora qui a [………] è la stessa di [………..]?"

9. **Asking about the Current Time:**

English: "What's the current time on your watch?"

Italian: "Qual è l'ora attuale nel tuo orologio?"

10. **Checking the Time for a Scheduled Event:**

English: "I have an event at [time]. Is it that time yet?"

Italian: "Ho un evento alle [,,,,,]. È gia' quell' ora?"

11.Inquiring about the Time of Day:

English: "Is it morning, afternoon, or evening right now?"

Italian: "È mattina, pomeriggio o sera in questo momento?"

12.Asking for the Time in a New Location:

English: "I just arrived. Can you tell me the local time?"

Italian: "Sono appena arrivato/a. Puoi dirmi l'ora locale?"

13.Requesting the Time Politely:

English: "May I ask you for the time, please?"

Italian: "Posso chiederle che ora è, per favore?"

14.Checking the Time for Transportation:

English: "I need to catch a train. What time is it?"

Italian: "Devo prendere il treno/. Che ora è?"

15.Inquiring about the Hour on a Clock:

English: "On the clock over there, what time does it show?"

Italian: "Sull'orologio laggiù, che ora indica?"

16.Asking for the Time with Gratitude:

English: "Thank you for your help. What time is it now?"

Italian: "Grazie per l'aiuto. Che ora è adesso?"

17.Requesting the Time from a Friend:

English: "Hey, can you tell me the time, buddy?"

Italian: "Ehi, puoi dirmi che ora è, amico?"

18.Asking the Time when you are in rush:

English: "It's getting late. Could you check the time for me?"

Italian: "Si sta facendo tardi. Potresti controllare l'ora per me?"

19.Inquiring about the bus departures:

English: "What time the bus will leave from here?"

Italian: "A che ora l' autobus parte da qui?"

20.Asking politely when the metro and train station will close:

English: " Excuse me; what time Metro/Train station will close today?"

Italian: "Scusami; a che ora la statzione della Metro/Treno chiude oggi?"

These phrases should help you communicate effectively when you enquiry about the time in Italy.

Chapter 13) DEAL WITH EMERGENCY CASES

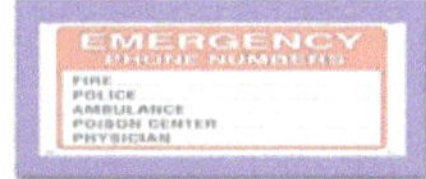

Here are 20 phrases in Italian that you might find useful when dealing with emergency cases:

1. Asking for Emergency Services:

English: "I need to call an ambulance. Is the number is 112?

Italian: "Devo chiamare un'ambulanza. E' il numero 112?

2. Reporting an Accident:

English: "There has been an accident at [location]."

Italian: "C'è stato un incidente a [.......]."

3. **Providing Your Location:**

English: "I am at [address/location]."

Italian: "Mi trovo in [……]."

4. **Describing the Situation:**

English: "There is a medical emergency. The person is [brief description]."

Italian: "C'è un'emergenza medica. La persona è […………]."

5. **Requesting Police Assistance:**

English: "I need to report a crime. Please send the police."

Italian: "Devo denunciare un crimine. Per favore, inviate la polizia."

6. **Providing Details:**

English: "The situation involves [details]."

Italian: "La situazione coinvolge [……..]."

7. **Reporting a Fire:**

English: "There is a fire at [location]."

Italian: "C'è un incendio a […….]."

8. **Providing Information about Injuries:**

English: "There are injuries, and medical assistance is needed."

Italian: "Ci sono feriti e serve assistenza medica."

9. **Confirming Safety:**

English: "I am in a safe location now."

Italian: "Mi trovo in un luogo sicuro adesso."

10. Describing a Dangerous Situation:

English: "The situation is dangerous. Please hurry."

Italian: "La situazione è pericolosa. Per favore, affrettatevi."

11. Requesting an Ambulance:
English: "I need an ambulance. It's an emergency."

Italian: "Ho bisogno di un'ambulanza. È un'emergenza."

12. Providing Contact Information:

English: "You can reach me at [phone number]."
Italian: "Mi potete contattare al numero [……….]." (Note: a quick Italian numbers reference to memorize, can be found at the last page of this book.)

13. Confirming Details:

English: "The emergency involves [details]."

Italian: "L'emergenza riguarda [………]."

14. Reporting a Missing Person:

English: "I need to report a missing person."

Italian: "Devo segnalare una persona scomparsa."

15. Requesting Assistance for Someone Else:

English: "I am calling on behalf of someone else who needs help."

Italian: "Chiamo a nome di un altra persona che ha bisogno di aiuto."

16. Inquiring about help Arrival Time:

English: "How soon can help arrive?"

Italian: "Quanto presto può arrivare l'aiuto?"

17. Providing a Description of the Perpetrator:

English: "The person responsible looks like [description]."

Italian: "La persona responsabile assomiglia a [.......]."

18. Cooperating with Authorities:

English: "I will cooperate fully with the authorities."

Italian: "Collaborerò pienamente con le autorità."

19. Expressing Urgency:

English: "This is an urgent situation. Please act quickly."

Italian: "Questa è una situazione urgente. Per favore, agite velocemente."

20. Expressing Gratitude for the quick help:

English: "Thank you for your prompt assistance."

Italian: "Grazie per l'assistenza tempestiva."

These phrases can help you to communicate in case of any emergencies in Italy. Note:(In Italy, the numbers for police, medical emergency, and fire fighters is the same for al of them , which is "112".)

The numbers that you need
 on your stay in Italy:

ZERO	0	ZERO
ONE	1	UNO
TWO	2	DUE
THRE	3	TRE
FOUR	4	QUATTRO
FIVE	5	CINQUE
SIX	6	SEI
SEVEN	7	SETTE
EIGHT	8	OTTO
NINE	9	NOVE
TEN	10	DIECI

These numbers will turn very useful in an emergency case or in an urgent reference, for example someone likes Hotels or Authorities could ask you, your mobile phone number, street number or number plate in case of any accidents could happen. This numbers template will be very practical when you find yourself in a strange situation.

THANK YOU